COMING TO AMERICA

A Muslim Family's Story

To Hassan, Soad, Amr, Dina, and Rowan.
Your courage, goodwill, natural courtesy, and simple honesty have refreshed my spirit.
I am honored to call you my friends.
— B.W.

Text and photographs copyright © 2003 by Bernard Wolf

LEE & LOW BOOKS Inc., 95 Madison Avenue, New York, NY 10016
www.leeandlow.com

Acknowledgments
I wish to thank the following people for their invaluable assistance during the preparation of this book: Mr. Ghazi
Y. Khankan, Director of Communications for the Islamic Center of Long Island; Ms. Magda Kamel, children's Arabic
teacher at the Islamic Center of New York; Ms. Jane Danapas, Principal of Intermediate School 10, Queens, New
York; Ms. Castro, sixth grade science teacher at Intermediate School 10, Queens, New York; Mr. Delmonte, Principal
of Public School 70, Queens, New York; Ms. Lisa DeGennaro, second grade homeroom teacher, and Ms. Denise
Cafarelli, second grade art teacher, at Public School 70, Queens, New York; and Ms. Linda Farhood-Karasavva,
professor of English at Hunter College, New York City. Finally, my special thanks to Louise E. May, the editor of this
book at Lee & Low Books, New York, for her patience, understanding, and for her brave sense of humor!—B.W.

Manufactured in China

Book design by Tania Garcia
Book production by The Kids at Our House

The text is set in Goudy Old Style

10 9 8 7 6 5 4 3 2 1
First Edition

Library of Congress Cataloging-in-Publication Data
Wolf, Bernard.
Coming to America: a Muslim family's story / by Bernard Wolf.— 1st ed.
p. cm.
Summary: Depicts the joys and hardships experienced by a Muslim family that immigrates to New York City from
Alexandria, Egypt, in the hope of making a better life for themselves.
ISBN 1-58430-086-8
1. Egyptian Americans—New York (State)—New York—Social conditions—Juvenile literature. 2. Immigrants—
New York (State)—New York—Social conditions—Juvenile literature. 3. Immigrant children—New York
(State)—New York—Social conditions—Juvenile literature. 4. Egyptian Americans—New York (State)—New
York—Religion—Juvenile literature. 5. Muslims—New York (State)—New York—Social conditions—Juvenile
literature. 6. New York (N.Y.)—Social conditions—Juvenile literature. [1. Egyptian Americans—New York
(State)—New York. 2. Immigrants—New York (State)—New York. 3. Muslims—New York (State)—New York.
4. New York (N.Y.)—Social conditions.] I. Title.
F128.9.E38 W65 2003   305.892'762073—dc21   2002067115

COMING TO AMERICA

A MUSLIM FAMILY'S STORY

BY **BERNARD WO**

LEE & LOW BOOKS INC. · NEW YORK

This is Rowan Mahmoud. She was born in Alexandria, Egypt, eight years ago. Now she lives and goes to school in America.

In Egypt Rowan's father, Hassan, was a social worker in a high school. Her mother, Soad, was an elementary school teacher. Between them Hassan and Soad earned only sixty dollars each month. This was not enough money to raise their family.

A year before Rowan was born, Soad read in the newspaper that the United States government was holding a green card lottery for Egyptians who wanted to work in America. A green card allows people from other countries to live legally in the United States. Soad and Hassan decided he should try to get one of these cards and then look for work in America. This would provide a chance for their growing family to find a better life.

When Rowan was two months old, her father finally received a letter saying he had won a green card! Hassan was thrilled, but then he became worried. How could he leave his wife alone with three young children?

Soad told her husband that with the help of their many relatives who lived nearby, she would manage. Soad then telephoned a cousin in New York City who owned a small grocery store. He agreed to give Hassan a job.

And so Rowan's father came to America without his family. For four lonely years he struggled to send as much money as possible to Soad.

Life in New York was *so* expensive, and finding a decent apartment seemed almost hopeless. But Hassan was a determined man. Through hard work and long hours, he slowly began to earn enough money to bring his family to live with him. Finally Hassan was also able to rent a modest apartment in Queens, with good schools nearby.

A few months later the family flew to America. Rowan was reunited with a father she did not remember but a father she quickly came to love and admire.

Here in his family's American home, Hassan thinks of himself as a rich man. All his struggles have been for his wife and children. He is still struggling, but with his family now by his side, all the sacrifices seem worthwhile.

Rowan's thirteen-year-old brother, Amr, is a thoughtful, intelligent boy who hopes to become an airline pilot.

Her twelve-year-old sister, Dina, is quiet and serious. She wants to become a children's doctor.

Rowan, with her quick wit and inquisitive mind, would like to be a teacher like her mother was in Egypt.

Soad is a patient, warmhearted woman who binds the family together with her love and constant care.

After only four years in this new land, the children speak English like Americans. Even Hassan almost does. Soad, however, is having a harder time. She studied English when she was a student but has forgotten most of it. Worse yet, her children speak only Arabic, their native language, to her.

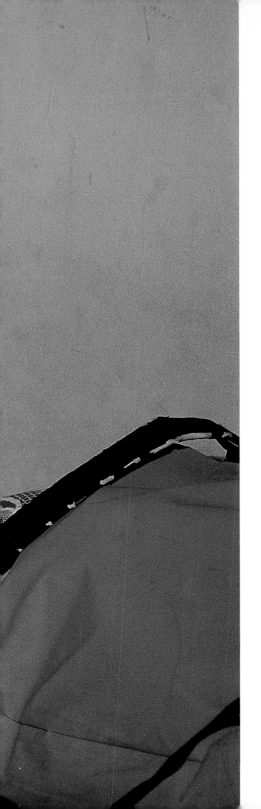

Soad reminds her children that tomorrow is a school day, and she shoos them away to do their homework. While Dina helps Rowan with a literature question, their parents are at their afternoon prayers in the living room.

Rowan's family is Muslim. Muslims are followers of Islam, a religion based on the belief in one God, who is called Allah. Muslims are required to pray to Allah five times each day in order to maintain their relationship with Allah throughout the day.

Muslim children do not have to pray until they are ten years old. When Rowan was seven, Soad began to teach her about Islam. This instruction comforts Rowan and helps her feel close to her family. Dina has been learning about Islam for several years, and she prays with her mother as often as she can.

Soad wants her children to learn about and practice their faith, but she also understands the importance of a good education. While her children are young, Soad helps them find ways both to honor their religion and become well educated.

In the back of the apartment, Amr works on a social studies assignment. He has a heavy load of classes and school activities, but he also makes sure to pray every day when he gets up and before he goes to bed.

In Alexandria Amr and Dina studied English in school. Rowan, always eager to learn new things, began to pick up the language from her brother and sister. Knowing English was a big help to the three of them when they arrived in New York.

Rowan is in the second grade at Public School 70, two blocks from her home. In today's art class everyone is making Father's Day cards. The children are given stiff sheets of paper with the outline of a necktie on one side. They are free to create their own designs on the tie.

Next to Rowan, Hany an Egyptian boy, suggests different colors for her tie. Rowan doesn't want to be rude. She thanks Hany but continues to follow her own ideas.

When Rowan is finished, she brings her design to her teacher. Ms. Cafarelli approves and gives Rowan scissors to cut out her tie. On the other side Rowan writes a greeting to her father.

At the end of the day Rowan's homeroom teacher, Ms. DeGennaro, reads a picture book to the class about a boy with a special father. Rowan can hardly wait to give her own special father the Father's Day card she's made for him!

Amr is in the eighth grade at Intermediate School 10, where students from forty-nine nations are enrolled. For Amr, school in America is a lot easier than it was in Egypt. There, the schoolwork was much harder and the teachers were very strict. If students misbehaved or did not learn their lessons, they were struck across their hands with a wooden cane.

In today's math class everyone is given a plastic device and a sheet of paper on which half an object

is drawn. When the device is placed where the drawing ends, the missing half of the object can be seen, and the class is challenged to draw it. This is an exercise in how to draw right angles. The tricky part is to look through the device at exactly the *right* angle.

After lunch in the cafeteria Amr goes to the school yard for a fast game of handball. His school in Alexandria did not have a cafeteria. The children brought their lunches and had only fifteen minutes to eat before going to their next class. Here, Amr has forty-five minutes for lunch and play—plenty of time to burn up some energy!

Dina is in the sixth grade at the same school as Amr. For Dina school in New York is also very different from school in Egypt. In Egypt girls and boys were taught in separate hot, overcrowded classrooms, and teachers demanded complete obedience. Here, there are only twenty-five to thirty students in each class, and every student has his or her own desk. Dina's teachers are friendly and encouraging, and they never use physical punishment.

Dina is surprised to see ten brand-new computers when she enters her science classroom. Ms. Castro tells the class she will show each student how to use them. When Dina's turn comes, Ms. Castro explains that the computers are programmed to help solve science problems and provide quick access to research material. Ms. Castro shows Dina how to look for the information she needs. This is going to be fun!

In the afternoon Dina and Amr pick up Rowan at her school and together they walk home. Soad is preparing the family's main meal of the day. Because Hassan works nights in a twenty-four-hour grocery store, he is still asleep.

Rowan and Dina pitch in to help their mother in the kitchen. In this way Soad teaches her daughters to cook the traditional foods of Egypt, just as her mother taught her. Rowan enjoys helping her mother, and she likes learning to cook. Meanwhile, Hassan wakes up, showers, shaves, and gets dressed for work.

The apartment's small front room serves both as the living room and dining area. Between two sofas there is just enough space for a large cocktail table. This is where the family eats its meals.

At 4:00 P.M. Soad covers the table with steaming dishes of delicious food. There is soup, chicken prepared two different ways, beef with vegetables, stuffed grape leaves, spicy ground beef kabobs, rice, and salads. Most Americans would see this as a feast for a special occasion, but Soad prepares such meals every day, following the Egyptian custom of enjoying a variety of tastes at each meal. Besides, there are five hungry people to feed!

Soad will pack part of the leftover food for Hassan's supper at work. She and the children will eat the rest for their nighttime meal.

Hassan's face shows the strain of his work schedule. He has only one hour for his meal and the company of his family. At 5:00 P.M. he leaves home for a ten-minute walk to the subway station. There he takes a train to Manhattan and then a bus to the store where he works.

After Hassan leaves for work Soad slips into a white gown and head covering, places a small prayer rug on the floor, and kneels on it to perform her afternoon prayers. She does not recite her prayers aloud. Hers is a silent communication with Allah. She knows that Allah can see into her heart and hear her thoughts. She is very worried about Hassan. He has been looking more and more exhausted. Soad prays for his health and safety.

Hassan arrives at the grocery store at 6:00 P.M. After eight years he knows every aspect of this business. His easy way with customers has earned good profits for his boss, but Hassan pays a heavy price. He is on his feet for twelve hours each night, six nights a week. Worst of all, he hardly has any time to spend with his family. When Hassan comes home from work at 7:00 A.M., his children are getting ready for school. There is only enough time to join them for breakfast. Then he performs his morning prayers and goes to bed.

Hassan feels guilty that the job of raising the children rests mostly on Soad's shoulders. But Hassan has a dream. One day he will have his own business. Then he will move his family to a larger apartment and buy them the things they cannot now afford.

After their meal Amr usually plays ball with his friends, and Rowan and Dina watch television for about an hour. Rowan enjoys watching children's programs and learning more about what is new and popular in America.

Rowan has adjusted well to life in New York. She has gotten used to the hot, steamy summers and cold winters. Rowan had never seen snow before—it is always too warm in Egypt. Now, like most children, Rowan has fun playing in the snow!

Monday is Hassan's day off, and in the afternoon he and Soad shop for food and staples. They live in a multiethnic neighborhood that includes a small Muslim community. On one street there are shops that specialize in Middle Eastern foods.

Soad and Hassan's first stop is a Muslim butcher who sells halal meat. Halal meat comes from animals whose blood has been completely drained off after slaughter. Muslims eat only halal meat, and they never eat pork. They feel pigs are dirty animals not fit for food.

In a shop next door Soad buys an Arabic newspaper. She's about to leave, but a case of luscious, freshly baked pastries catches her eye. She can't resist! She splurges and buys five pieces of baklava as a special treat for her family.

Their last stop is a small supermarket where Hassan and Soad load up on sale items and other foods they need for the week: onions, rice, green vegetables, fruit, milk, and juice. There is also a good selection of Middle Eastern delicacies, and the prices are lower than at the specialty shops. Soad is a careful shopper. Every dollar she spends must go as far as possible.

At 9:00 A.M. on June 18 Amr and his entire eighth-grade class assemble in their caps and gowns to claim their reward for three years of hard work. It's graduation day!

Hassan and Soad sit with an uncle of Amr in the packed balcony. Hassan has come straight from his night's work.

After speeches from school officials, teachers, and the school's principal, the big moment finally arrives. To loud applause and cheers from parents and the other students, the graduates go up onstage one by one. When Amr's name is called, he walks forward to receive his diploma. He is modest about his excellent grades, but it feels good to know he's done well.

The celebrations continue. Sunday, June 27, is Amr's fourteenth birthday. Everyone agrees to have his birthday party the next day so Hassan can be there too.

On Monday night Amr greets his guests as they arrive. He wears the one gift he's been longing for—an Italian soccer jersey. Soad and Hassan haven't forgotten their son's quiet hints.

Amr's guests are his best friend, Victor, and Mariana, a girl who graduated with him. Rowan and Dina have invited their best friend, Dania, who lives nearby.

Soad carries in Amr's birthday cake, sets it down in front of him, and lights the candles. Everyone sings "Happy Birthday," and they cheer when he blows out all the candles with one breath.

Rowan watches eagerly as her mother slices portions of the cake. Yummy! Strawberry shortcake—her favorite dessert!

Later Soad brings out her video camera and asks everyone to take a turn posing with Amr. They all agree happily. Soad is grateful because the happiest person at the party is Hassan. It is *so* good to see him relaxed and full of laughter.

Now that the children are finished with their school year, Soad decides to do something about all the English she has forgotten. On Saturdays she goes to Manhattan's Hunter College, where she takes a class in English for foreign adults. It's comforting to be with a group of people who are also struggling with English.

Soad's teacher, Professor Karasavva, encourages the class not to be embarrassed or afraid of making mistakes when speaking English. Most people are helpful, she says, and will appreciate the efforts they make when trying to communicate in a language that is new to them.

It's been a long time since Soad was a student. Now not only is her English improving slowly, but she is having fun!

Rowan, Dina, and Amr love their summer vacation. They sleep late in the morning and stay up later at night. They don't have homework to do. And best of all, they spend lots of time with their friends.

This afternoon, Amr and Victor play one-on-one basketball. They use the traffic stop sign for a basketball hoop. When the ball hits the sign, it's a score. Victor is a good athlete, but he has a tough time getting the ball away from Amr, who is *very* quick.

Meanwhile, Rowan and Dina spend time with some Greek friends who live down the street. Rowan stands apart from the group, strangely silent.

Sonia, an older girl, asks Rowan if she is all right. Rowan just nods. Sensing that something is troubling her young friend, Sonia holds Rowan in a soft hug.

Sometimes memories of her life in Alexandria come rushing back to Rowan. She misses her neighborhood, where everyone knew everyone else. She misses the excitement of festive holidays. She misses the long, golden beaches just a few streets away from where she lived. Most of all she misses the many friends she left behind and her large, loving, extended family.

Hassan has told Rowan that he will try to take the family back to Egypt for a visit one summer. Rowan understands how costly that would be. She never reminds him of the trip.

Before Rowan, Dina, and Amr return to school in the fall, Hassan and Soad take them to worship at a beautiful mosque in Manhattan. On a Friday in late August, they visit the great mosque for afternoon prayers. Friday is the holiest day of the week for Muslims. It is their Sabbath.

People remove their shoes before entering the mosque and leave them in cubbyholes provided for this purpose. Rowan and Dina are given head coverings. Muslim women are required to cover their heads when they are in public or in the presence of men other than family members. It is a sign of modesty.

From the doorway Hassan sees that the mosque is crowded with worshipers, and Soad wonders where they will find places. Hassan must leave for work as soon as prayers are finished, so he suggests they all go to the farthest end of the mosque, where there is some open space.

Once inside, Hassan and Amr bow, then kneel and press their heads to the carpet. They face east, toward Mecca. Mecca is the city in Saudi Arabia where the prophet Muhammad was born. Facing east is a gesture of respect for Muhammad, the man who wrote the Qur'an, Islam's holy book.

Rowan sits with her mother and Dina in silent prayer near the back of the mosque, away from the men. This is an ancient Islamic tradition. Women and men are separated so the men are not distracted from their prayers by the beauty of women.

The mosque does not have an altar or paintings or sculptures of any living creatures. Under Islamic law it is forbidden to honor idols or statues. Instead worshipers face a wall that is covered with geometric patterned Persian tiles. Rowan feels comforted by the closeness of her family and all the people who pray in this beautiful place.

As their prayers conclude, Hassan glances fondly at his son. He and Soad have much to be grateful for. They are well pleased with their children. After Allah, it is they who are the truest treasure of their lives.

AFTERWORD

In recent years a new wave of immigrants has come to the United States from countries in the Middle East, Africa, Asia, Europe, and South America. These new immigrants are Muslims. Like others before them, they come seeking a better life for themselves and their families. It is estimated that today there are between five and seven million Muslims in America, and about two billion Muslims worldwide.

Muslims are sustained by their faith in Islam, an Arabic word meaning "submission." Islam requires complete submission to Allah, the one true God, and total acceptance of Allah's final teachings as revealed by his prophet, Muhammad, in the seventh century A.D. and recorded by Muhammad in the Qur'an, the holy book of Islam. The Qur'an is the source for Islamic religion and morality. The Qur'an also emphasizes the importance of family and provides guidance for the conduct of everyday life.

There are five basic religious duties, or pillars, that all Muslims must practice. The first pillar requires reciting a prayer that declares Allah is the only God and that Muhammad is his prophet. The second obliges Muslims to offer prayers to Allah five times each day. This inspires followers to a higher morality, purifies the heart, and prevents temptations toward wrongdoing. The third pillar requires those who can to give approximately 2-1/2 percent of their annual income to the poor and needy in their communities. The fourth requires fasting from sunrise to sunset during the month of Ramadan—not as punishment, but to teach wisdom, patience, and discipline. The fifth pillar calls for a pilgrimage to the holy city of Mecca at least once in each Muslim's lifetime, except for those who are too poor or too ill to make the journey. This pilgrimage is the culmination of a Muslim's religious duties.